This book belongs to

_____

Oprah Winfrey

By Mary Nhin

Illustrated By
Yuliia Zolotova

This book is dedicated to my children - Mikey, Kobe, and Jojo.

From an early age, my life was tough. I was born into a very poor family and we moved around a lot.

The only place I felt safe was at my father's house. My dad was strict, so I had to pay attention in school and study every day before dinner.

When I was old enough, I got a job reading the news on the local radio.

I loved to talk and, surprisingly, people seemed to love to listen to me.

This made me want to use my voice to make a difference and, possibly, make it a career. I decided early on that one of my goals was to win a college scholarship.

I joined drama and debate clubs and I even entered speaking contests to add to my experiences. This helped me win a scholarship and I had the chance to study at Tennessee State University.

Once I graduated, I got a job on television, co-hosting the news.

I was the FIRST ever black woman to host on the show and the youngest member of the whole crew. Boy, I was proud!

It felt like a dream come true, but some people never gave me a chance. When the show failed, I got all of the blame.

My boss took me off TV and sent me to write reports instead. I was so sad.

I couldn't just give up. I had worked hard to get here. I just had to believe in myself.

You don't become what you want,
you become what you believe.

So, I decided to do something about it. I tried again. I left that job and joined a talk show. Almost immediately, the show rocketed from the bottom rank to the top. The audience loved it so much that the producers renamed the show *The Oprah Winfrey Show*.

The biggest adventure you can ever take is to live the life of your dreams.

Timeline

1976 – Oprah becomes co-anchor on television news

1977 – Oprah was removed from the television role
        and given a reporting role

1983 – Oprah joins struggling talk show AM Chicago

1986 – The talk show is renamed *The Oprah
        Winfrey Show*

minimovers.tv

 @marynhin   @GrowGrit
#minimoversandshakers

 Mary Nhin   Ninja Life Hacks

 Ninja Life Hacks

 @ninjalifehacks.tv

Lightning Source UK Ltd.
Milton Keynes UK
UKHW051025010323
417763UK00011B/58

* 9 7 8 1 6 3 7 3 1 3 8 5 5 *